Aliens in NYC

Nemir Matos Cintrón

www.editorialatabex.com

Poems © 1996, 1998, 1999, 2000, 2014 Nemir Matos Cintrón

Diseño del libro: Yolanda V. Fundora / www.TowardADigitalAesthetic.com

Foto de Nemir (página 36) © David Renteria

Reservados todos los derechos. Prohibida la reproducción total o parcial de esta obra sin autorización escrita de los titulares de los derechos.

These poems were written in NYC. They are photographic in that they portray a slice of life of immigrants from Latin America and the Caribbean. They are autobiographical in a vicarious way since I share with these immigrants both my cultural identity and sense of estrangement from mainstream culture.

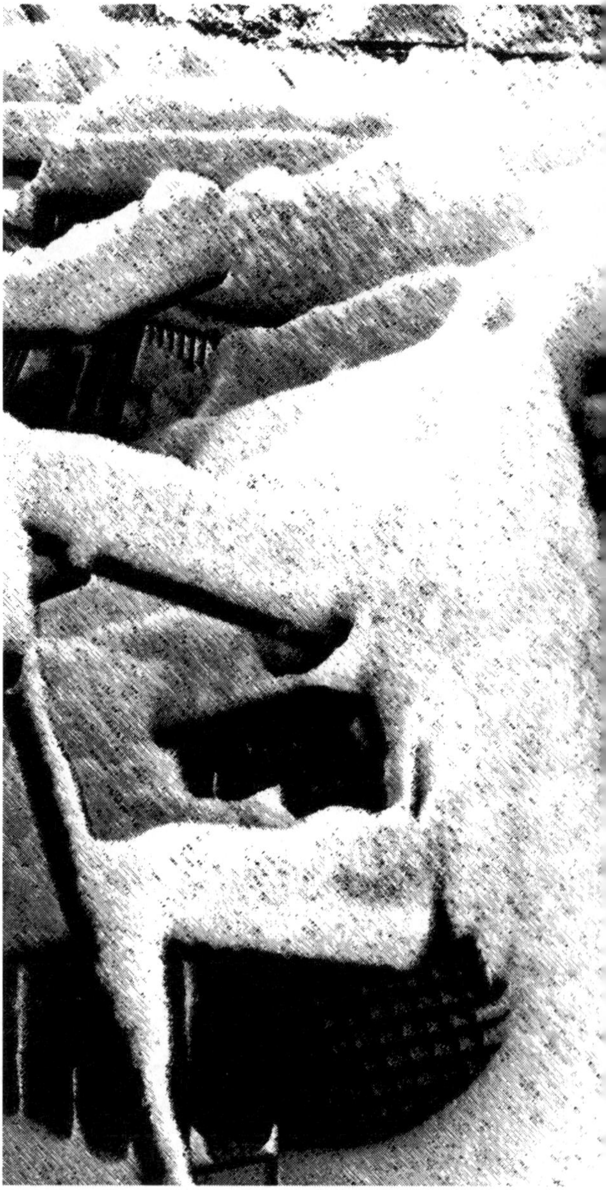

México Lindo en la 116

¡Señita...tamales...atole...pozole!
rugged hands ...*arrugadas manos*... like an ancient map
from a lost sanctuary
her rugged hands... a desert
creases flowing like rivers through the sand
overflowing misery left behind.
From the lost ceremonial city of the heart...
chiclipote, zopilote, guajolote..! turkey
fleeing from the butcher's hand
with no thanksgiving to celebrate
after that long pilgrimage from Tucumani or Puebla
A shopping cart turned *comal* under the snow
Her rugged hands clapping tortillas by the fire
¡Señito, tamalito, compre...buy!
to return home down south across the border
Poverty left behind
and newfound poverty of El Barrio
in the East Side
of Upper Manhattan...
¡A Peso Tamales, Atole, Chimichangas compre Seño, buy..!
to go back
from the wrinkles ...of her hands...
creases not attended by the laundry girl
who works from nine to nine fearful of the migra
a new arrival in Manhattan.
¡Nopalitos con queso blanco!
overflowing cactus soft and tender after plucking
the thorns...of the mind.
Nopalitos with moist white cheese from a distant cow
south of the border, milked under the Aztec moon.
Empty smile of long gone teeth...
but smiling any way

selling *Tamalitos* to return to Puebla or Tucumani
under the snow, wrapped her heart with the *rebozo,*
curling tight by her *comal,* fire under the snow.
Señita Tamales Atole Pozole! pudgy rugged hands
that have never seen a Korean Nail parlor
decorated with Harina de maiz, the original corn meal
to make tortillas
almost as if singing lullaby... *¡Linda manita tiene la nena..!*
looking at the moon inside her heart...
milking that distant cow of Tucumani...Puebla...Potosi
a shopping cart turned comal...fire under the snow...
her rugged hands.

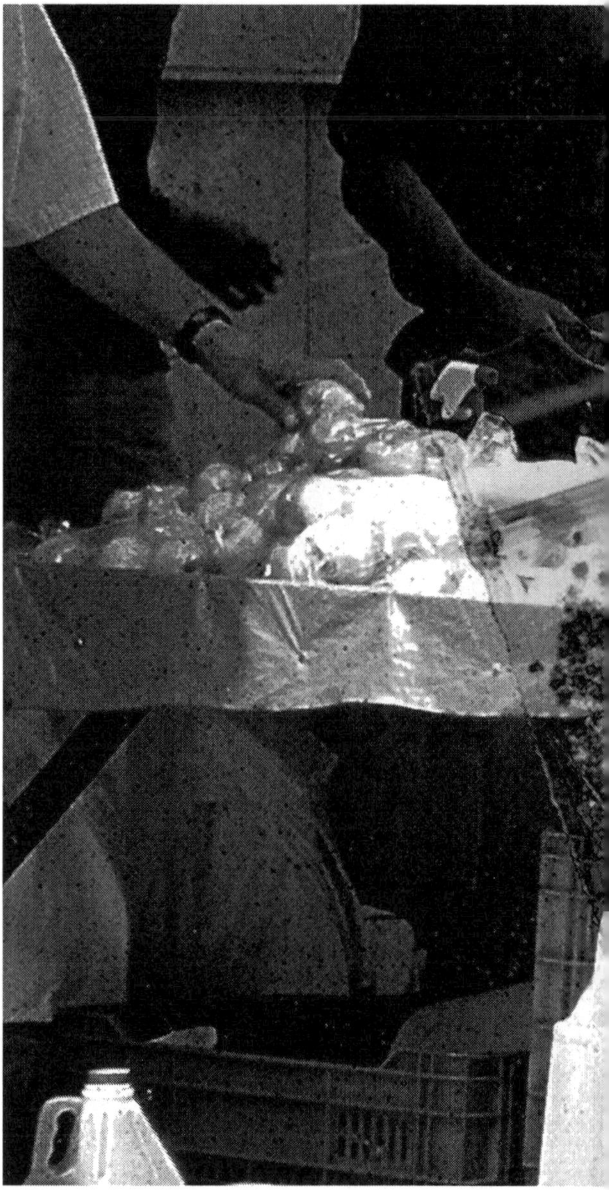

La Vereda Tropical

Facing the Hudson river.. blaring music…merengazo, oozing
from apartment buildings in the Upper West Side
of another island called Manhattan.
Scoring Mangú con queso , soft mashed plantain
in La Vereda Tropical
not a country trail but a little restaurant
on 168 & Broadway in Quisqueya Heights.
Old photographs hanging from the walls,
a faded tropical landscape behind a couple holding hands,
eyes squinting from the blinding sun of
La República Dominicana,
campesino country music from a Quisqueya left behind
bachata melodies flooding senses with tropical nostalgia
of love forlorn and forgotten by a true vereda tropical,
a distant country trail still damp with memories
of love and betrayal
now made songs and old pictures
covered with New York grime and dusty
grease from Queso frito.
There is no Trujillo here in Quisqueya Heights
It's another civil war
distant from the one left at home after 1961.
it's only Cadenú counting his drug money
a stack of twenties under the counter top
while he talks about the benefits of working out.
Only crack, crack, crack cocaine
dictates the traffic in the alleys,
it's **crack, crack, crack** cocaine and sleepy Heroin trying to forget
a far off boat cracking under a tropical moon
cracking before reaching sister shore of Puerto Rico
never reaching New York City.

But no, there is no Trujillo here or Balaguer, never been
no dictator ever in Quisqueya Heights
save Envíos Nacionales, sending money to return

to the newfound democracy of Dominican Republic of today
to return someday to be somebody but nobody
for the smell of the Bodega, a pungent smell of onions
rotting under the summer heat of New York City
passes on in the handshake of the Bodeguero trying to pass
for paisano..middle class..upon return
back in that other island of Quisqueya
far beyond Quisqueya Heights.

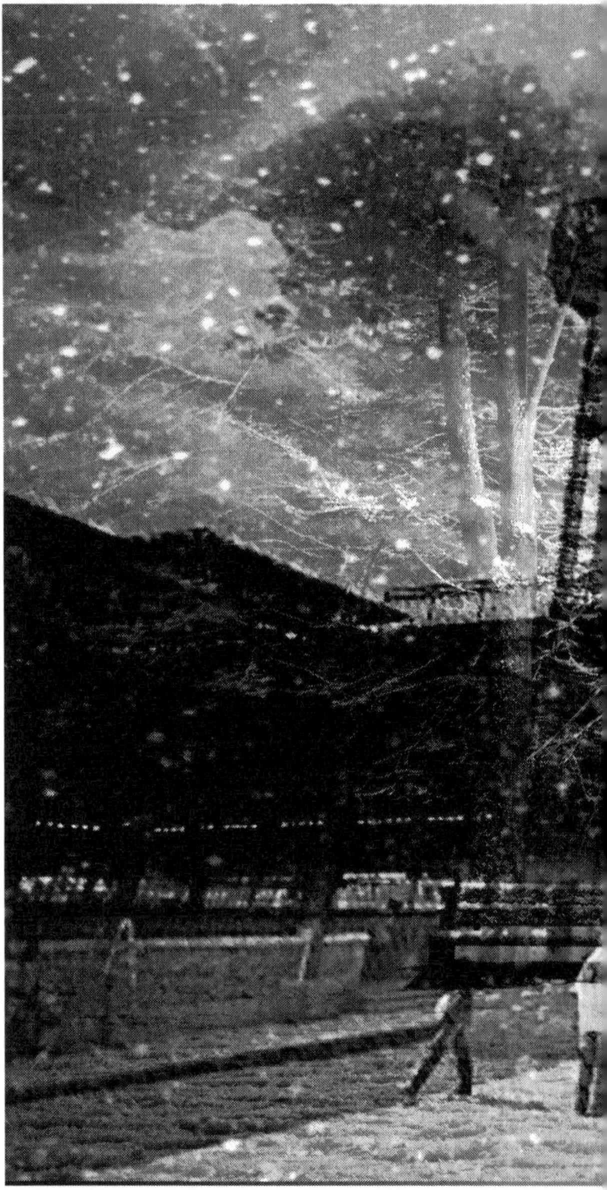

Haitian Market under the Snow

Ma Tine folds and unfolds her humanity
red turban nesting her black head
folds of blackness are her arms folded under the falling snow
Ma Tine peddles peanuts, cinnamon, nutmeg
and herbs unknown
to simple eyes
accustomed to buy McCormick Spices
on a shelf in the supermarket...
Who are her real clients?
Jamaican cooks and Puerto Rican doñas
who really know how to cook jerk chicken and *arroz con dulce?*
Metropolitan hougans casting a spell...?
Dieu qui decide
Ma Tine folds and unfolds her humanity
red turban nesting her black head
her eyes gazing through the snow
as if waiting for the Lwa, or the Laplas:
the restless messenger of the Ougan
to buy from her the serpent oil
for Damballah, the spirit of change...
and here they come...
coiling and recoiling...
swirls of snow forming *veves* on the sidewalk:
ritual drawings of the lwas
Papa Legba, ouvri bayé por nou
sings Ma Tine in rapture
unfolding her blackness under the white snow
forgetting for a moment where she is at
looking at the landscape of her mind..back in Haiti
sitting in the Iron Market...the Mache Fé...
side by side the peanut brittle vendor
Praline...Praline...

Papa Legba, ouvri bayee por nou
asking to the Lwa to open the roads
that never-ending road back home to the Rada
nation of spirits.

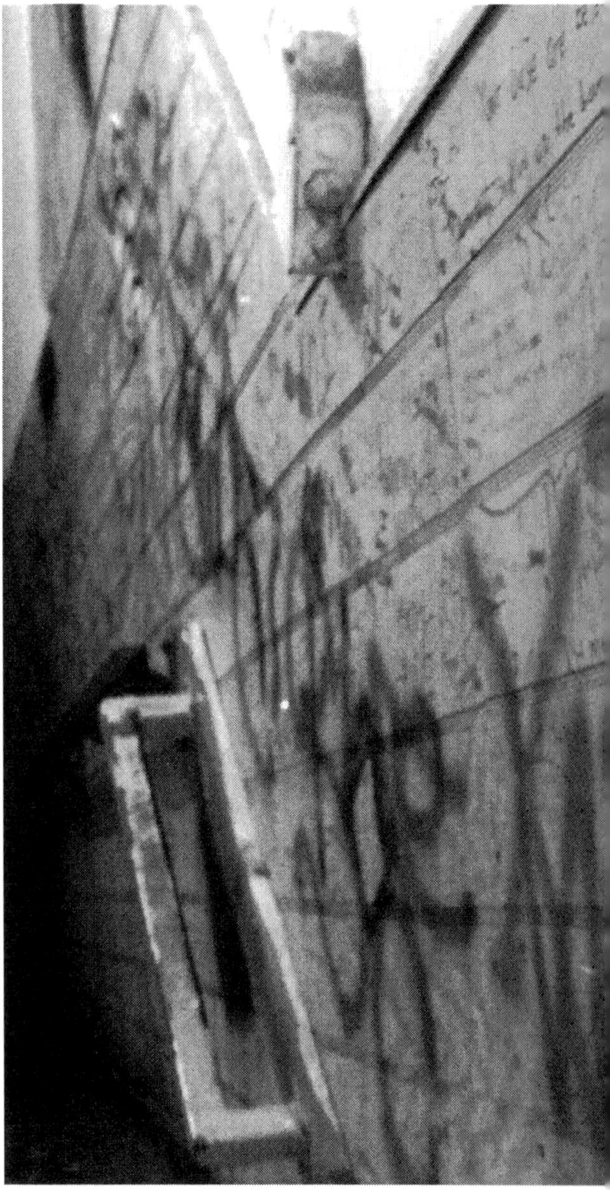

De la Patagonia al Subway

From the highlands of Peru
to the underworld of New York City... El Condor Pasa
Pied pipers, subway charmers: flautistas de Amelín;
haunting melodies pierce through
the underworld of Grand Central Station
from the highlands of Peru
stretching to southern Patagonia,
flute dreams of solitary landscapes
syncopated by the wailing of sea lions
and whales mating at night
under the glaring luminance of the aurora australis.

From the highlands of Peru to the North
where everything is better
lured by a dream of abundance... El Condor Pasa
Always dreaming to return to the pueblito but always leaving
Pronto volveré, ya me voy, ya me estoy yendo

Pied pipers, subway charmers: flautistas de Amelín,
from the underworld of New York City's subway;
dark tunnels resonate a tapestry of colors
woven by the diligent hands
of young women from the highlands of Peru
dreaming of the better life of "El Norte".

Ten living in a studio, selling sweaters on the subway,
harassed by the police
that was never mentioned on the journey
from the highlands of Peru
to the underworld of New York City
Always dreaming to return to the pueblito but always leaving
Pronto volveré, ya me voy, ya me estoy yendo

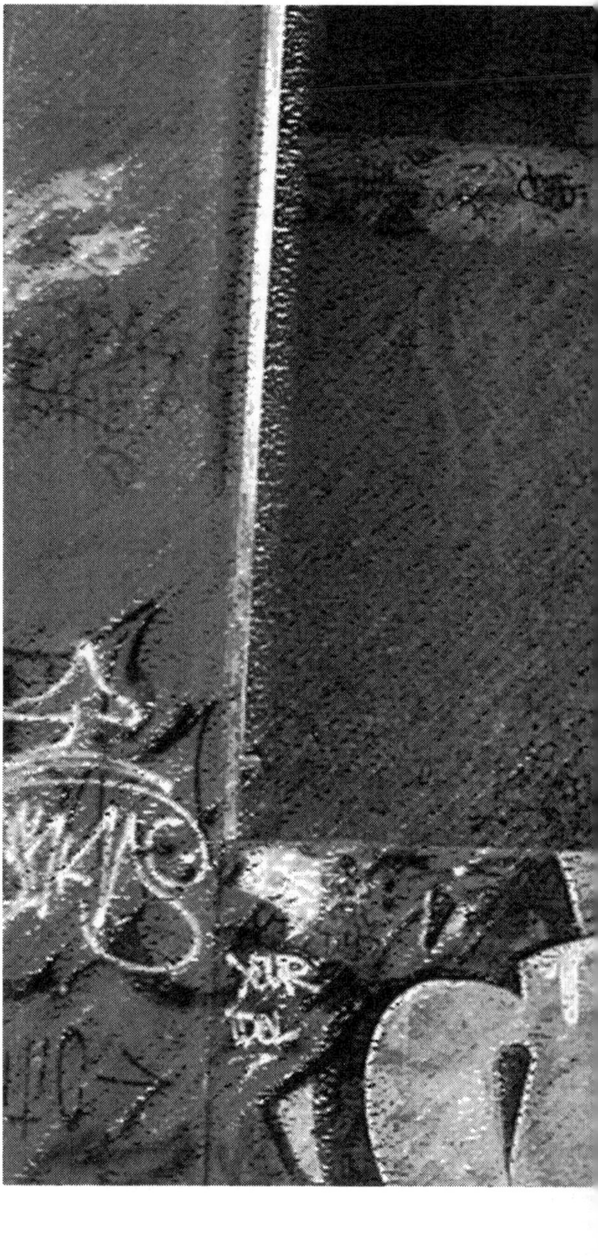

Marcelino No Bread No Wine

Manicured lawns of Long Island northern shore,
a true postcard
of the American Dream.
Gold Coast east of New York City
home to the Morgan's, the Woolworth's and the Pratt's
the "true Americans";
a postcard
now soiled with walking graffiti: pedestrians in Suburbia
disturbing the symmetry of landscapes
designed by Italians
but tendered by Salvadorian, Ecuadorian
and Nicaraguan domestics
toiling by day
hiding under tarps at night.
Marcelino sin pan ni vino
Marcelino no bread, no wine
a man curled up like a baby under the freeway of Glenn Cove.

Open spaces, single-family homes:
bedroom communities of yesteryear,
squeaky cleaned today by Salvadorian, Ecuadorian
and Nicaraguan domestics
scrubbing by day
but listening at night
to the wailing sound of a man crying like an abandoned baby
they cannot nurse to sleep under the freeway of Glenn Cove.
Marcelino sin pan ni vino
Marcelino no bread, no wine.

Manicured lawns of Long Island northern shore,
a graying postcard
of the American Dream.
bedroom communities of yesteryear,
now empty nests as Baby Boom turned Baby Bust.
Seniors fed and Depend changed
By Salvadorian, Ecuadorian and Nicaraguan home attendants
who could not keep alive a man dying like an oversized baby
under the freeway at Glenn Cove.
Marcelino sin pan ni vino,
Marcelino no bread, no wine.
'cause in the Gold Coast east of New York City
home of the Morgans, the Woolworth's and the Pratt's,
the "true Americans";
nobody according to the sound bite of his brother on TV
nobody here on Earth but only in heaven
could take good care of him
where he lays safe and nested in the arms of God.

Based on a true story of Salvadorian worker Marcelino. 1997

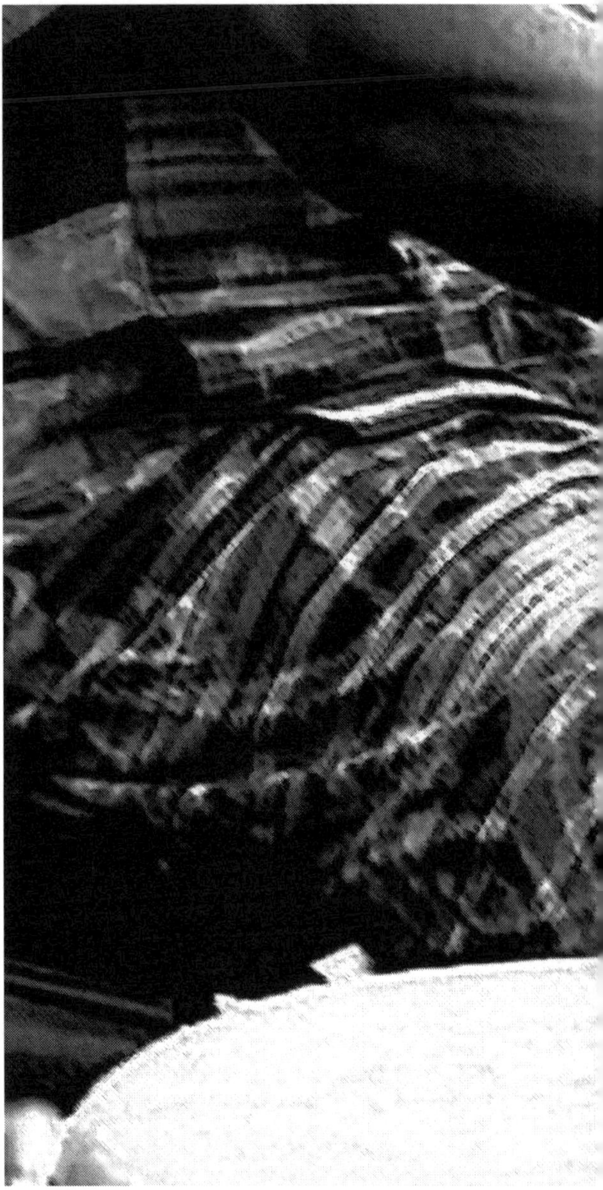

Revisiting Cuban poet Nicolás Gillén's poem:
Todo Mezclado

Licking your black armpits of dreams forgotten
now remembered under the
jungle beneath your navel,
I find myself swimming in turquoise waters
of the West Indies.
Sounds of Yoruba drums resonate in my temples
as I taste the rhythm between your legs.
Indian smells of cinnamon and
curry overflow my senses,
as I lift my head from your deep sea
to see your face in rapture.
Three hills greet me:
the first one,
erupting volcano on my tongue,
the other two sway at a distance as I,
a true conquistador reaching your
shore, rename you Trinidad.
Fierce Carib armies in your hands
hold my body captive under yours
as if dancing to the music of *parangs*
brought from Venezuela as *parrandas*
Feel my fingers dancing gently for you now,
no Spanish soldiers to ignite your wrath
and propel your arrows.

It must be, love, that you can taste in me
that same Spanish blood which
conquered your ancestors
It must be, love, that I'll never forget
sweet nothings you whispered in my ear
in the language of the master.
You and I, both "esclavo" and "señor"
master and slave
in this journey of sweat,
sweet and sour chutney, pasta de guayaba
English breakfast tea, café con leche,
horseradish and ground garlic,
Todo mezclado: *mangú, mofongo, calalú*
a mixture, a mélange of smell, sweat
and sap from our bodies
molten under a fake tropical sun
painted on a wall
behind my bed in New York City.

Nemir Matos Cintrón

Born in Puerto Rico on November 19, 1949. She has published three collections of poetry: *Las Mujeres no hablan asi, A traves del Aire y el Fuego, pero no del Cristal (1981)* and *El Arte de Morir (2014)*. Her poetry is included in various anthologies both in Puerto Rico and in the United States. She lives in the United States since 1993 working in the field of instructional design in higher education.

Other books by Nemir Matos Cintrón.

Las Mujeres No Hablan Así

El Arte de Morir y La Pequeña Muerte